Spring Changes

ISBN 0-439-36833-2

Text and photographs copyright © 2002 by Ellen Senisi.
All rights reserved. Published by Scholastic Inc.
SCHOLASTIC, CARTWHEEL BOOKS, and associated logos are trademarks and/or registered trademarks of Scholastic Inc.

Library of Congress Cataloging-in-Publication Data available.

12 11 10 9 8 7 6 5 4 3   03 04 05

Printed in the U.S.A.
First printing, March 2002

Spring Changes

by Ellen B. Senisi

SCHOLASTIC INC.

New York Toronto London Auckland Sydney
Mexico City New Delhi Hong Kong Buenos Aires

For Cass, remembering the spring of a thousand peach blossoms,
and for Moises, a superstar!
—E.S.

What's one of the first signs of spring? Pussy willows!
You know spring is coming when you see
their soft, grey buds pop out into the chilly air.

The weather is still cold from winter. The sun is slowly warming up the earth. Except for evergreens, other trees and plants are still bare and brown.

Daylight lasts longer and longer.

The weather keeps changing. It can be snowy or rainy or windy or sunny—maybe even all in the same day!

Snow melts. Rain falls. There is mud and dirt everywhere.

Water and sunlight help roots and seeds grow into plants.
The new plants will grow right through the dirt and into the open air.

Like magic, plants change and grow!

Leaf buds push their way out of woody branches.

The buds unfold slowly into bright, green leaves on trees and bushes.

More buds form as flowers get ready to open up and bloom.

Some flowers bloom
early in spring.

Others bloom later
in spring.

Soon the spring air is warm and inviting, and many flowers
open wide to the rain and sun.

In spring, warm weather means we don't need coats or boots.

People plant gardens in the spring. It's exciting to watch plants grow—especially ones you will be able to eat later!

There's a feeling of excitement in the warm, sunny air.

Outside is the only place you want to be.

Look around—
living creatures are
suddenly everywhere.

Some wake up after sleeping through the cold winter.

Others come alive for the first time in spring.

Many come back after going south for the winter.

Many baby animals are born in the spring.

They want to run and play like people do.

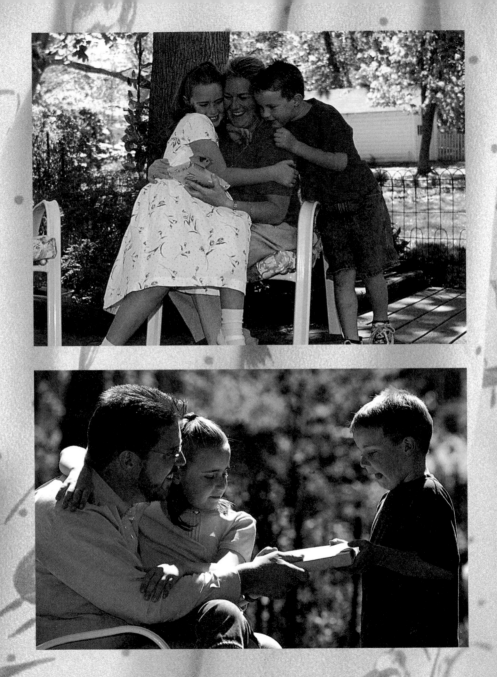

People celebrate spring holidays. There's Mother's Day and Father's Day.

Some families celebrate Passover or Easter.

But, most of all, people welcome new life and sunny warmth in spring.

Look around and see . . . spring changes are everywhere!

Soon, with barely a whisper, spring slips into summer.